Katy Perry
One of the Boys

Album Artwork: © 2008 Capitol Music Group, a division of Capitol Records, LLC
Management: Direct Management Group, Inc./Bradford Cobb, Martin Kirkup & Steven Jensen
Special Thanks to Blue Hamilton and the A & R/Creative Team at Warner Chappell Music

Alfred Publishing Co., Inc.
16320 Roscoe Blvd., Suite 100
P.O. Box 10003
Van Nuys, CA 91410-0003
alfred.com

ISBN-10: 0-7390-5684-0
ISBN-13: 978-0-7390-5684-4

Contents

ONE OF THE BOYS

Words and Music by
KATY PERRY

Moderately fast ♩ = 138

12

I KISSED A GIRL

Words and Music by
KATY PERRY, LUKASZ GOTTWALD,
MAX MARTIN and CATHY DENNIS

I Kissed a Girl - 4 - 1
31810

Bridge:

Us girls, we are so mag-i-cal,___ soft skin, red lips, so kiss-a-ble.___

Hard to re-sist, so touch-a-ble.___ Too good_ to de-ny__ it.___

D.S. % al Coda

Ain't no big deal, it's in-no-cent._____ (Ooh.___)

Coda

I liked___ it. (Ooh._____)

WAKING UP IN VEGAS

Words and Music by
KATY PERRY, ANDREAS CARLSSON
and DESMOND CHILD

Moderately ♩ = 126

Verse 1:

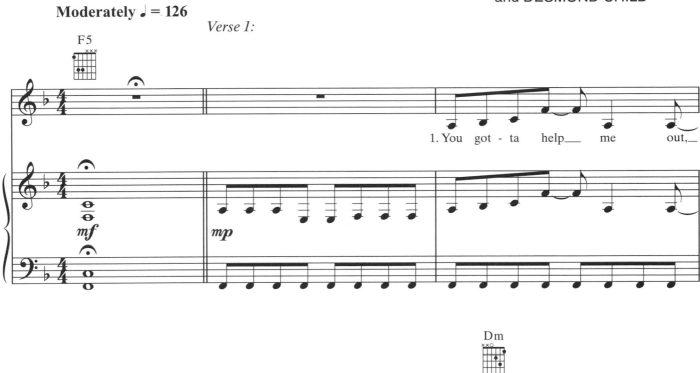

1. You got - ta help__ me out,__

it's all a blur__ last night.____

We need a tax - i 'cause you're hung - o - ver and I'm

Verses 2 & 3:

Bridge:

Shake the glit - ter,   shake,   shake,__ shake the glit -

ter.   1. Gim - me some cash   out,
2., etc. *(Instrumental)*

ba - by.__   Gim - me some cash   out,   ba - by.__

Repeat ad lib. and fade

THINKING OF YOU

Words and Music by
KATY PERRY

Slowly ♩ = 76

Verse 1 (sing 1st time only):

1. Com - par - i - sons are eas - i - ly done_ once you've

Verse 2 (sing 2nd time only):

(2.) In - di - an sum - mer in the mid - dle_ of win - ter, like a

mp

(with pedal)

had_ a taste of per - fec - tion. Like an

hard_ can - dy with a sur - prise cen - ter. How do

Chorus:

26

MANNEQUIN

Moderately fast ♩ = 132

Words and Music by
KATY PERRY

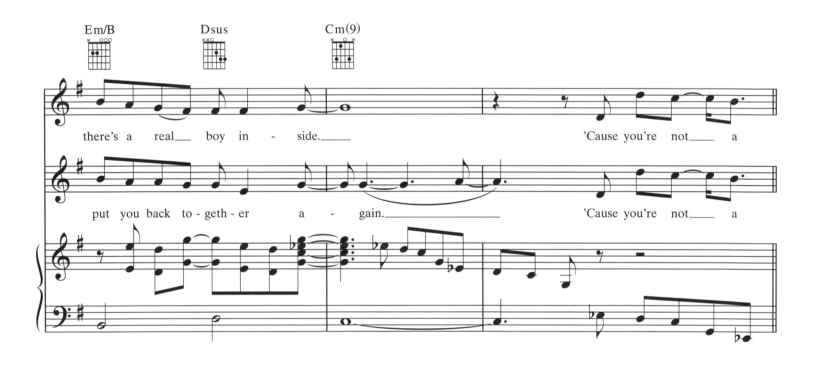

UR SO GAY

Words and Music by
KATY PERRY and GREG WELLS

Ur So Gay - 7 - 1
31810

Verse 1 (sing 1st time only):

Verse 2 (sing 2nd time only):

1. I hope you hang your-self_____ with your H & M

2. You're so sad, may-be you should buy a hap-py meal.___

scarf, while j***-ing - off,_____ lis - ten - ing to Mo -

_____ You're so skin-ny, you should real - ly su - per-size the deal.___

zart. You bitch and moan_ a - bout L. A., wish-ing you were in the rain, read-ing Hem-ing-way.

_____ Se - cret-ly you're so a-mused that no - bod-y un-der-stands you.

Chorus:

HOT N COLD

Words and Music by
KATY PERRY, LUKASZ GOTTWALD
and MAX MARTIN

Moderately fast ♩ = 132

Verse:

1. You change your mind___ like a girl___ chang-es clothes.___
2. We used to be___ just like twins,___ so in sync.___

Yeah, you PMS___ like a bitch.___
The same en-er-gy___ now's a dead___

I would know.___ And you o-ver-think,___
bat-ter-y.___ Used to laugh 'bout noth-ing.___

48

IF YOU CAN AFFORD ME

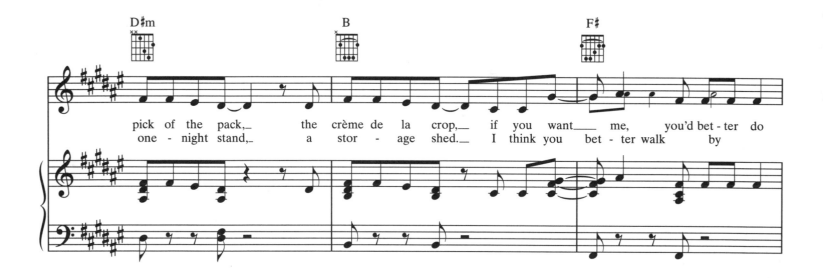

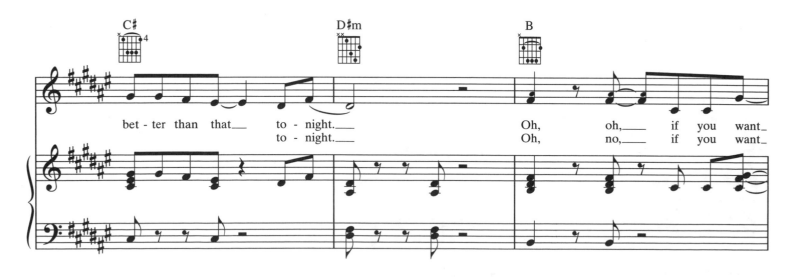

If You Can Afford Me - 6 - 1
31810

Chorus:

pay___ the___ bill 'cause that's___ the
noth - ing's___ free, ex - cept___ lov - ing me.

deal.} If you wan-na ride,___ just name your price,___ and

don't play cheap with___ your heart. Don't make a bet___ if you can't write the check_

for me,___ for me.___ 'Cause I can be

LOST

Words and Music by
KATY PERRY and TED BRUNER

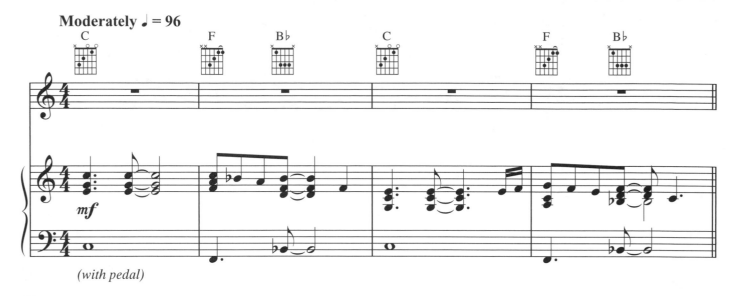

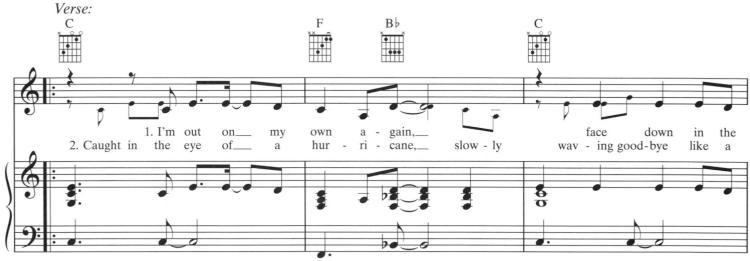

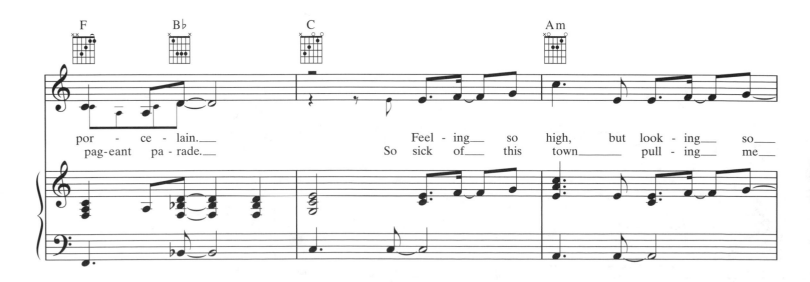

SELF INFLICTED

Words and Music by
KATY PERRY, SCOTT CUTLER
and ANNE PREVEN

Chorus:

been bro-ken, but my heart is still wide o-pen.
of e-mo-tion. My heart rips me wide o-pen.

I___ can't stop, don't care if___ I___ lose.___ Ba-by,

you are the weap-on I___ choose._ These wounds are self - in - flict - ed.___

I'm___ go-ing down in flames_ for___ you.___ Ba-by,

Self Inflicted - 5 - 2
31810

I'M STILL BREATHING

Words and Music by
KATY PERRY and DAVE STEWART

1. I leave the gas___ on, walk the al - leys in the dark.
2. May - be I was too pale, may - be I was___ too fat.

Sleep with can - dles burn - ing, I leave the door un - locked.
May - be you had bet - ter, bet - ter luck in___ the sack.

I'm Still Breathing - 5 - 1
31810

FINGERPRINTS

Words and Music by
KATY PERRY and GREG WELLS

Moderately fast ♩ = 132

Verse:

N.C.

1. Vot - ed most like - ly to end up on the back of a milk - box drink.

Looks like I'm let - ting 'em down. _____ 'Cause

G2   Asus

sev - en sev - en - ty - five _____ is - n't worth an ho - ur of my
2. Rep - re - sent - ing you _____ and _____ me, don't you wan - na go down _____ in

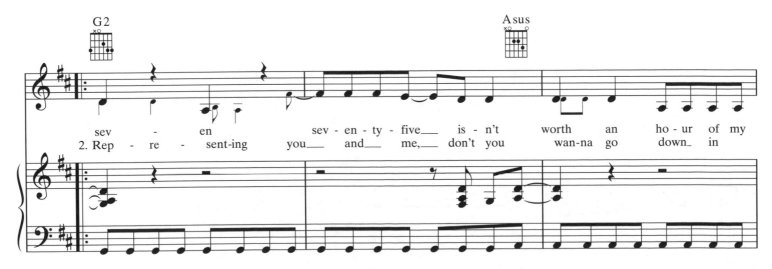

Fingerprints - 7 - 1
31810

74

Half-time feel

Bridge:

Don't _____ give up, _____ but

don't _____ give _____ in. _____ Build your house _____

on the rock, _____ oh, _____ not in _____ the sand, in _____ the sand, in

cresc.

the sand, in the sand.

Chorus:

It's my life, and I'm not sit-ting on the side-

lines, watch-ing it pass me by. I'm

leav-ing you my leg-a-cy. I got-ta make my mark,